PEOPLE THROUGH HISTORY

PEOPLE HAVING FUN

by Karen Bryant-Mole

WAYLAND

PEOPLE THROUGH HISTORY

People in the Country
People in the Town
People at Home
People at Work
People Having Fun
People On The Move

First published in 1996 by Wayland (Publishers) Ltd.,
61 Western Road, Hove BN3 1JD, England.

© Copyright 1996 BryantMole Books
Edited by Deborah Elliott
Designed and Typeset by Chrissie Sloan
Cover designed by Liz Miller

British Library Cataloguing in Publication Data
Bryant-Mole, Karen
People Having Fun- (People Through History Series)
1. Title II. Series
306. 4810941
ISBN 0 7502 1827 4

Printed and bound in Italy by G. Canale & C.S.p.A.

Contents

Going to the circus

Animals were once the main attraction of a circus. Nowadays, human performers amaze and delight audiences.

1890s

Circuses travelled around the country. As they came into town, people lined the road to watch the elephants with their colourful riders and all the other circus animals and performers.

1940s

These children are watching as a man puts up posters for a visiting circus. The posters advertised performing lions, bulls, bears, tigers and horses.

Now

Today, most people think that it is unfair to make wild animals do tricks and live in cages. Now, most of the acts in a circus are performed by humans.

Going on holiday

A hundred years ago, a holiday was often just a day trip to the seaside.
Today, many people have a two-week holiday and visit places all over the world.

1890s

These children have come to the seaside for the day. They are playing in the sand in their ordinary clothes. Swimming in the sea was still quite an unusual thing to do. Anyone who did swim would have changed in these bathing huts on wheels.

1950s

The most popular type of holiday was a week by the sea, somewhere in Britain. The beaches were often very crowded.

Now

Many people now fly off to holidays in the sun. These holiday-makers are having a relaxing time on a beach in Greece.

7

Christmas

Christmas Day is celebrated in many countries of the world. Lots of the things to do with Christmas are traditional. That is, people have done them in the same way for very many years.

1910s

Father Christmas is on his way to visit these children in their school. He is carrying small presents and sweets in his sack.

1950s

These children had to spend their Christmas in hospital. The nurses helped them to have fun by arranging a Christmas party and a visit from Father Christmas.

Now

Presents have been part of Christmas for many years. Today's children often receive many more presents than children in the past.

Going to the fair

Years ago, fairs were places to buy and sell animals. Today, people go to fairs to ride on huge rollercoasters and other exciting attractions.

1890s

Fairs were usually held in a town once a year. Animals were bought and sold and farm workers could be hired. There were stalls and side shows, too.

1930s

Most fairs were fun fairs. People went along to go on rides and have a good time. Fun fairs were usually travelling fairs that went from town to town.

Now

Amusement parks are fairs that stay in the same place all year round. There are lots of different rides. Some people enjoy being scared on rides like this!

Children's games

Today's toyshops have thousands of toys and games for children to choose from. In the past, children made up their own games or played with simple toys such as dolls or trains.

1890s

Games such as leapfrog, marbles and skipping were very popular. Children often played outdoors, in the streets surrounding their houses or in other open spaces.

1930s

This little girl is taking her dolls for a ride in their pram. The pram looks like a small version of the prams that mothers pushed their real babies around in.

Now

There are many children's toys and games to choose from. Lots of children enjoy playing computer games. This boy is having fun with a walkie talkie.

Sports Day

In the past, people often competed for medals and cups at Sports Days. Today, they usually compete to collect points for their team instead.

1910s

Sports Days were not just for children. Everyone in the village could take part. This man is having a go at the high jump during a village Sports Day.

1930s

One of these boys is about to land with a splash. His friend has knocked him off a greasy pole. This was part of a school Sports Day.

1950s

These children are competing in the 'All Fours' race. The winner and the children in second and third places received prizes.

Now

Everyone is having fun at this school Sports Day. Today, many schools do not give prizes to the winners. Taking part is just as much fun as winning.

At the seaside

People have always enjoyed holidays and day trips to the seaside. Nowadays, there are more rides and amusements to entertain people.

1890s

The ladies in this picture are riding their donkeys side-saddle. They sat with both legs on the same side of the donkey. All the people are dressed very smartly for their visit to the seaside.

1930s

Children loved Punch and Judy puppet shows. The puppeteer would set up a stall on the beach and children would gather round to watch the fun.

Now

There are merry-go-rounds, helter skelters and other rides to entertain children at the seaside. There are cafés and stalls where food can be bought and amusement arcades with games.

Dancing

People have been going to dances for hundreds of years. The music and dances have changed a lot. Today's disco dancing is very different to the ballroom dancing of the past.

1930s

Many dances were formal dances. The men wore suits with bow ties and the women wore long dresses. A band played music for dances like the waltz and the foxtrot.

1950s

Rock and roll music became popular during the 1950s. It was a new type of music with new dances, such as the jive. The boy at the front is wearing clothes called Teddy boy clothes.

Now

Disco dancing is enjoyed by people of all ages. Discos have flashing lights and loud, fast music. People dance on their own or with friends.

Royal celebrations

Many people like to join in with the celebrations on days that are special for the royal family. There have been royal weddings, birthdays, coronations and jubilees.

1890s

This procession was held to celebrate Queen Victoria's diamond jubilee in 1897. She had been queen for sixty years. Lots of the children are holding flags.

1910s

George V was crowned as king in 1911, at a ceremony called a coronation. This is one of the huge coronation bonfires that were built around the country in celebration.

1950s

This tea party was held to celebrate another coronation. It was the coronation of Elizabeth II, who is still our queen today.

Now

The queen's official birthday takes place in June. She celebrates the day by taking part in a ceremony called the Trooping of the Colour. It is watched by lots of people.

Swimming

Years ago, people swam in cold rivers and lakes. Today's swimming pools have warm, clean water. Many pools have special shallow areas for babies.

1910s

These people are bathing in a river. Swimming was not as popular as it is today. Few people swam in the sea.

1930s

As swimming became more fashionable, swimming pools began to be built. Many were built next to the sea. An open air pool, like this one, was sometimes known as a lido.

Now

Most of today's pools are under cover. Some of them have wave machines or water chutes, which make swimming even more fun.

Going to the park

Parks were once just open spaces that people could visit. Today, most parks have children's playgrounds with swings, slides and rides.

1890s

People enjoyed going for walks in this park. There is a band playing in the bandstand. Lots of people have stopped to listen to the music.

1950s

Children used to come to this park every day, after school. The slide was very popular.

1970s

This rocking horse was set into concrete. If children fell onto the concrete, they sometimes hurt themselves very badly.

Now

This play area has wood chippings on the ground. They are much safer then concrete. Today's playgrounds often have exciting things to climb on and explore.

May Day

The 1st of May is also known as May Day. The celebrations are connected with springtime. They have been held near or on this day for many hundreds of years.

1890s

These children are about to perform a maypole dance. They would have danced around the maypole, weaving the ribbons into a pretty pattern.

1950s

The girl who is seated is being crowned as the May Queen. The older people who are watching probably took part in a ceremony like this when they were young.

Now

Many children still take part in traditional May Day celebrations, held on the first Monday in May. These children are dressed in special costumes.

In the snow

On snowy winter's days, people still build snowmen and go sledging as they did in the past. Some people now have fun in the snow on skiing holidays.

1890s

These men are playing a winter game called curling. They slid the large curling stones along the ice towards an iron pin. Whoever was nearest the pin won.

1910s

These boys look ready for action. They are holding snowballs in their hands. The little boy on the left is being pushed along on a wooden sledge.

1940s

During extremely cold winters the ice on rivers can become thick enough to walk, skate and play on. It is very unusual for ice to be this thick.
Never try to walk on ice yourself.

Now

Some people go on skiing holidays. Children, too, can learn to race down the snowy slopes. One of these children has goggles to protect her eyes from the bright sunshine.

Glossary

advertised   let people know about

amusement arcades   places where there are lots of games machines

attractions   things or places that people come to see

celebration   a special occasion

ceremony   a set of actions that people perform

compete   try to win

coronation   the ceremony at which a king or queen is crowned

ferry   a small ship that carries people and vehicles

jubilee   a celebration for a particular number of years

puppeteer   a person who controls puppets

traditional   has happened in the same way for years

Books to read

History From Objects series by Karen Bryant-Mole (Wayland 1994)

History From Photographs series by Kath Cox and Pat Hughes (Wayland 1995-6)

How We Used to Live 1954-1970 by Freda Kelsall (A&C Black 1987)

Looking Back series (Wayland 1991)

Acknowledgements

The publishers would like to thank the following for allowing their pictures to be used in this book: Beamish, The North of England Open Air Museum 4, 6 (and cover), 7 (left), 8, 9 (left), 10,11 (left), 12, 13 (left), 14 (both), 16, 17 (left), 18, 19 (left), 20 (both), 21 (left), 22, 23 (left), 24 (both), 25 (left and cover), 26, 27 (top), 28 (both), 29 (left); Cephas, Clive Platt 15 (right); Chapel Studios/Zul Mukhida, 5 (right), 19 (right), John Heinrich 13 (right), 25 (right), Adam Good 29 (right); Eye Ubiquitous, Roger Chester 11 (right), Paul Seheult 17 (right), (cover); Hulton Deutsch 5 (left), 15 (left); Positive Images 7 (right); Topham Picture Source 23 (right), Brian Gibbs 27 (bottom); Zefa 9 (right), 21 (right).

Index